GH00792143

"Like the title of this book, 'Songs for the Journey', this collection signifies a journey in itself. It charts the interior voyage, from despair to a hope-filled experience which is both future and now. But also, individual poems are like resting places to pause and reflect on what is my experience, what do I really want, what is important to me and how do I get to where I want to be? These poems are thoughtful, thought-provoking and worshipful – they encourage us to stay hopeful, because, as the poet says: 'All that is now is not all that there is / All that will be / Is far more / Than the heart could imagine.'"

SARAH FORDHAM

Marketing and Communications Co-ordinator of Integral, a global alliance of Christian relief and development agencies. Sarah is a church leader in north London and an author and poet, whose published works include 'Psalm Readings', 'Love's First Touch' and 'In the Cool of the Day'.

SONGS

for the

JOURNEY

A collection of poems
about the epic journey
that is life

BARBARA TODD

 Zaccmedia

Published by Zaccmedia
www.zaccmedia.com
info@zaccmedia.com

Published December 2019

ISBN: 978-1-911211-87-7

British Library Cataloguing-in-Publication Data
A catalogue record for this book is available from the British Library.

Front cover photograph:
Old Harry's Rock, Dorset, © *2018 Will Van Wingerden*

Back cover and interior section photographs:
Old Harry's Rock, Dorset, © *2018 Jose Llamas*

CONTENTS

FOREWORD

The Old Testament Psalms were designed for careful and thoughtful reflection – some specifically whilst on pilgrimage to Jerusalem. So Barbara's title for this collection of poetry follows a sound tradition! Her measured choice of words and phrases, which echo many Biblical passages, needs to be absorbed in that same, considered way. They form a modern parallel to those writings of David (and others) in facing up to issues that impact us deeply. Barbara's sensitive unpacking of those resultant struggles, forms a prelude to pointing us to a better way – a spiritual journey alongside 'The One who holds all things together'. This collection is commended as an "unfolding" of the truth. Culminating in the fourth section, which underlines the reality of our destination and relationship with God, these *'Songs for the Journey'* are a supportive element in perceiving what that means, and how it's achieved.

STEPHEN BISHOP

Premier Praise Radio broadcaster, 'The Way' website contributor, and author of numerous books and Bible teaching resources, including 'Dialogue with a Donkey' and 'Two Minutes Added On.'

ACKNOWLEDGEMENTS

Thank you to all who have supported and encouraged me along the way, and, to those, in particular in the various congregations of the London based Ichthus Christian Fellowship, who have given me the opportunity to read my poems, from both this and my previous collection, The Stones are Still Singing, at various meetings and events, and to those individuals who have used my poems at dance workshops, group reflections and church retreats. Thanks also to Paul Stanier from Zaccmedia and Stephen Bishop, who've encouraged me to keep on writing and publishing, and to Will Watson, for his help in proof-reading and editing the text, and in writing the introduction.

I dedicate the poem 'Hope' to the Ichthus church plant, Hope Church Mitcham, and the poem 'Battle', to my own church, Southcroft Church, Streatham, for which it was written.

INTRODUCTION

This new collection of poems has been inspired by the current social climate, in which, I believe, at least in western culture, a sense of unhappiness seems to be increasngly prevalent – with a feeling that who we are, what we have and what we have achieved is never good enough. These observations led me to consider what the root of this could be, and what could be done to overcome it.

Social media, for example, invented so that we can better connect with our friends and family, seems to be producing a deep seated unhappness, particularly amongst the young, driving many to dissatisfaction with self-image and personal life. Much of this seems to be because it is so often used to portray something as near perfect as possible, with the editing out of parts of life, or self-image, that people don't want others to see.

I believe that, as humans, we have an innate desire to be happy. When we aren't, or, at least, when we don't think that we measure up to the expected standards of what constitutes this happiness, we start to look at ourselves and begin to ask what is wrong with us. We are constantly surrounded by advertisements that push this – that there is something wrong with us, and we should be unhappy with our current state of affairs – promoting, for example, the next and best solution to fix all of our human defaults. Whether it's a new car to increase our social status, or a new dress that gives us a bit more confidence, we're told that 'things' will make us happier. This focus on 'things' promotes the idea that the more we have, the happier we will be. I think, generally speaking, that many of us fall victim to this: we associate happiness with material possession. It's not hard to see why, then, social media is littered with people posting about all the things they have, and it's also not hard to see why we imagine that these people are happy.

Unfortunately, however, these 'things' never do make us truly happy. Ask yourself this: can you think of one material possession, that you bought, say, ten years ago, that contributes to your happiness now. Does that ten year old material thing still bring you peace and contentedness? I believe that very few people would answer the latter question with a resounding yes. The reason for this, is that joy in a material possession fades away – it serves only as a temporary boost to happiness.

Songs for the Journey poses questions around where our true happiness should lie. It considers dilemmas and situations that affect us, addressing some of today's pressing issues, such as problems that the internet, social media and mobile phones generate, which might be of interest to young people and schools, possibly being a springboard for discussion and reflection. The poems challenge us to rethink our lives, pointing out that it's never too late to have a fresh start. Some have an obvious spiritual focus, or are based around New Testament parables and Christian ideals, and so could be used in church meetings, or school assemblies and RE lessons.

Songs for the Journey has a number of recurring motifs, such as light and darkness, hope and singing, the latter also being a particular focus of my first of book of poems, The Stones are Still Singing. I offer it to you trusting that you will find some of it, at least, challenging or inspiring, as you continue upon the epic journey that is life.

The collection of poems has four sections:

A place of discord: the first section of the book presents some of the difficulties, obstacles and situations that many of us face in our lives and how these contribute to our unhappiness. Issues such as depression, isolation and rejection – sadly all too prevalent in this modern western world - are considered. My hope here, is to inspire the reader with a relatable insight into a few of these issues.

Defrosting slowly: the poems in this section seek to challenge us to think about where we are in life. To be happy and content, we must recognise the things in our lives that are not good, and then seek to move away from them. We must set ourselves on good ground and let our roots go deep. We must think about those who are around us – are they good for us, do they encourage us and do they have our best interests at heart? In order to move forward, into something better, we must be prepared to go on a journey of transformation.

Above all else: in this section of the book, the poems are based around a range of positive values and qualities. I believe happiness, at least in part, can be attributed to what we value above all else; instead of valuing things that fade away, we should focus on things that last, such as seeking wisdom, truth and forgiveness. This section also highlights personal charateristics that we should aspire to, such as being joyful, loving and patient.

When we prioritise these, we begin to see that they cannot be found in the acquistion of material possessions, or immediate gratification: these are lifelong pursuits.

Glimpses of Heaven: the final section of this book is a selection of poems that introduces the reality of an invisible world – a heavenly realm. Many of us spend our lives focusing on the 'now', rather than contemplating what is to come. There is great joy, happiness and hope to be found in remembering, and in envisioning where we are ultimately heading. Based around the new Heaven and new Earth, as described in the New Testament book of Revelation, these poems seek to remind the reader that there is a long term goal of eternal happiness which is rooted in God.

A place of discord

Beginning

It all began in a garden
From beautiful fresh greenness
New life sprang
A place of peace
A place of growth
A place to walk in relationship
In the cool of the day
Everything that was needed
Was there
All that was needed to
Satisfy hearts, bodies and minds
But even so
Their restless spirits
Drove them to hunger
For what should not be
And to take
What they should not have
In beautiful fresh greenness
Death loomed
A place of discord
A place of loss
A place to hide away from the One
Who had loved them
From the beginning

Good Intentions

They say that the way is paved
With good intentions
The overflowing of hearts and minds
With purposefulness
Paving stones
Ablaze with hope
Resplendent with exciting prospects
Stretch into the distance
As far as the eye can see
Enticing us forward
But further on
As yet out of sight
Their bright colours fade
A dullness greys their dazzling intensity
Dashed on the rocks of disappointment
Aspirations fail
Sinking in the swamp of setbacks
Dreams shatter
Those intentions that once drove us onwards
Now weigh us down

Loss

Nothing can fill the empty spaces
The places
Where joy once reigned
Where laughter rang
Where love filled all
Was all in all
Your sight, your sound
Your smell, are found
No more
Your sweet caress
Your softest kiss
Are gone
Forever lost
Nothing can replace
Nothing refill
The gaping hole you left
Yet still
Your memory remains
A residue
Of so much good
And beautiful
Your ghost still walks
Deep in the heart
That still belongs
To you

Words

You have the key to my happiness in your hands
You have the power to make me laugh or cry
The words you utter
Could cause a song to rise in my heart
Or a dagger to pierce my soul
I wait
For those words
Which could make today
A day when my heart sings for joy
I hope
That today will not be
One when that same heart
Sinks, crushed and despairing
Do you not know
Are you not aware
Of the power you wield
Of the life-giving, life-affirming potential
Of the words you utter
Do not destroy my hope
Do not bruise my spirit
Do not tread on my dreams

Sadness

The sadness seeps in slowly, surreptitiously
Surrounding everything
Sinking it down, down, down
To a depth from which
It feels that nothing could possibly return
Its overwhelming weight
A pressure too hard to bear
A burden that cannot be lifted
A wound that will not heal
Such sadness is not easy to dispel
Such sadness hovers around
Lurking amongst laughter
Jeopardising joy
It dampens every hope of happiness
And chases away every source of solace
This sadness simply will not leave
Its lure of solitude, separating from succour
Remains as a residue
Even when the sun is shining

old

The person I see reflected back at me
Is not the person I am
Is not the person I know
This face I see
Is surely not
My face
Where have these lines
These wrinkles
These lumps, these blemishes
All come from
This heart, this mind
Have not changed with time
I am still
Who I always have been
But those who see me now
Do not know this
Cannot comprehend
That time has caused
Such deception
That it has stolen away
The knowledge
Of my true identity

Stuff

When I'm feeling down
Feeling low
A little retail therapy
Makes me feel much better
A pair of new shoes
A new dress
Always lifts my spirits
Always makes me feel
Much better
At least for a while

When I'm feeling bored
Feeling at a loose end
A little shopping trip
Makes me feel much better
A visit to the mall
A search online
Always lifts my spirits
Always makes me feel
Much better
At least for a while

But all this stuff
Is never enough
To block up the gaping holes inside me
Its accumulation
Cannot wipe away my tears
Blot out the tumult in my mind
Or still my troubled heart
That one more new thing
One more purchase
Does not bring me lasting joy
Enduring peace
More new stuff
Yet more stuff
Will not put my world to rights

Friends

Starting from scratch
A new account, a new page
Where to begin
Rummaging through reams
Of people I may know
Fifty friends
Editing profiles
Posting photos
Checking notifications
Two hundred friends
Scrolling through status updates
Repeating jokes
Reposting memes
Five hundred friends
Writing on walls
Clicking on likes
Adding more groups
A thousand friends and rising
Selecting quotes
Incorporating emojis
W a i t !
Do you actually like me
Do you really know who I am
Do you care whether
I laugh or I cry
How I'm feeling today
Can anyone really have a thousand friends

Click

Such power lies in only a moment's thought
A quick reaction
A second's touch
The power to build
Or to destroy
Like: unlike
To fuel joy: to enhance worthlessness
To instill purpose: to destroy dreams
With a click of a finger
Destinies are diverted
And reputations ruined
Waiting for the verdict
The judgement of a thousand eyes
Scanning the pages, the walls
The verdict of faceless harbingers
Bringing down destruction
On watchers
And counters, hoping for more
Desperately anticipating each affirmation
Every click piling up positives
Whilst dreading the possible devastation
Of disapproval

Accusation

The innocent suffer
Betrayed by those
Blind to injustice
Their falsehoods
A knife in the back
An arrow in the heart
Indelible words
Wreak damage, not easily mended
Blame apportioned
Where undeserved
Fashions smears, not soon forgotten
No thought of
A reputation sullied
A life in tatters
This vilification
Obliterates all expectation
Of a bright future
Destroys every anticipation
Of good things
Until all hope
Is extinguished

Rejection

I know they don't like me
Don't want me
Have rejected me
I can see it in their eyes
Read it in their body language
They stare at me
Eyeing me up
From top to toe
Scrutinising my appearance
Analysing every detail
They whisper behind my back
Criticise my every move
Blame me
For every problem
I don't conform
To their ideas
To their ideals
I don't fit in
I don't belong
I'm not needed
Not wanted
Here

Happiness

An expectation of happiness pervades everything
Its clamour blaring everywhere
Enticing us with promises
Telling us that
There's a wonderful life out there
If only we would grasp hold of it
Illusions of happiness deceive everyone
That all is well
That things are on the up
Thus everyone believes that
Everyone else is happy
Bombarded with images of perfection
Beautiful people who invade our screens
Peddling their thoughts
Their latest hacks
For every possible scenario
No time for self-reflection
To pause and consider
To analyse
For this goes against the grain
In this world where
Self-affirmation is the name of the game
The truth, that all may not, in fact, be well
That not everything can be perfect
Strikes a nerve
And is usually best avoided

Fear

Fear is a totalitarian tyrant
Subjugating all who stand in its way
Numbing minds
Paralysing bodies
Enshrouding hearts
Crouching patiently at the door
It waits for an opportune moment
Then creeps in stealthily
At first, unnoticed
Dragging with it a sense of misgiving
A burgeoning anxiety and apprehension
Fear surrounds its victims
With a feeling of foreboding
Seeding an anticipation of calamity
It descends like a lead blanket
Overpowering, engulfing
Suffocating, immobilising
Every thought
Every act
Until each quails in submission
Of its implacable will

Hooked

From its unremitting gaze
There is no escape
As it smiles upon me
I am drawn
Into its tight embrace
Compelled by the lure
Of its promise of a better day
I capitulate
Blind to its imperfections
Deaf to all contrary voices
I approach
And am again held fast
In its iron grip
I am ensnared
A slave to its incessant demands
For it cannot let me go
And I
Have been enthralled
Entrapped
It does not permit my release
I will remain
In need of rescue

Isolation

Silently sitting, all in a row, separate yet together
Side by side, yet all alone
Staring intently, totally absorbed
Slaves to tiny screens
Hearts and minds captured
By anonymous giants pulling strings from afar
Influencing, controlling, manipulating
Exiled from reality
Yet believing that this is where
Everything matters
No sound here
Other than the interminable tapping of fingers
The constant clicking of keys
They say you can be lonely
In a crowd
Here is a barren land
Devoid of true human kindness
Where invisible, silent voices
Angrily shout out their lies
Luring captives
Into desolate places
Where isolation calls the mind
To retreat further
Into its wilderness

Depression

These white-washed walls
Press savagely down on me
Nothing can lift
Their impenetrable darkness
Incarceration needs no prison bars

No room to move
No space to breathe
No gleam of light through
Their wide-open window
The sunshine outside is cold and thin
No warmth to thaw
The numbness of my soul
A brittle soul shattered
Its shards puncturing hope
Bleeding out every expectation
Of a new horizon
Sinking downwards
Corkscrewing inwards
To hidden recesses of emptiness
From that depth
No hand can pull me back
You cannot follow where I go

Brokenhearted

This heart is broken
It will not mend
Nothing can heal its sorrow
Close its gaping wound
Nothing can be spoken
That will bring
A way to ease
Its anguish
And its pain

This heart is broken
It cannot find
The joy in simple pleasures
The peace that calms the mind
Everything feels hollow
Numb, forlorn
Empty
And bereft
It pines alone

This heart is broken
For how long
Must it bear such desolation
And heaviness so strong
What could ease its sadness
Lift its grief
Nothing
Seems to aid
Or bring relief

Walls

These walls must fall
They must come down
For they have held us captive, bound
For far too long
Walls of hurt and anger
Panic, fear
Seem insurmountable
These walls our mountains
Of the mind
They trap us with their lies
And hold us fast
Immobilised
They threaten
Dominate our thoughts
And infiltrate our dreams
This illusion of
Imprisonment
Must be unmasked
Exposed at last
These walls must fall
They must come down

Defrosting slowly

I wish

I wish
That I could
Cradle your fractured heart
Gently, in the palms
Of my hands
Whisper to it softly
That love is not lost
Has not melted away
I wish
That I could
Wipe away your tears
With my hair
Bring joy to your face once more
Stop all that has punctured
This disconsolate heart of yours
Wounding it beyond words
That it might not bleed forever
I wish
That I could
Convince your anxious heart
That there is still hope to be found
That it waits
Just around the corner
Where a cornucopia of good things
Is lying
Ready to be unpacked

All things new

It is never too late to start over
Do not think that you are stuck
Where you are
How you are
Forever
For nothing has been completed
That cannot be restarted
Nothing is lost
That cannot be restored
Old things can be renewed
All things can be made new
So do not give up
Before you have barely begun
Believe that the seeming impossible
Is possible
There is hope
There is always hope
For all things can be made new
The One who holds all things together
Holds you in His hands
Your name is engraved on His palms
He who created all things
Can make all things new

Come near

Those who have a heavy heart, come near
For those who feel burdened
Will be clothed in joyful praise
Those who are weary, come near
For those who are exhausted
Will soar as if they had wings like eagles
Those who have lived in fear, come near
For those who are afraid
Will be able to stay in the place where God is
Those who are bound in chains, come near
For those who have been long held captive
Will know freedom forever
Those who are dry and empty, come near
For the hungry and thirsty
Will receive bread and water from the Living One
Those who walk about in darkness, come near
For those who cannot see
Will come into the Light of the World
For now, now is the time of favour
Now, now is the time
To purchase what cannot be bought
To seize hold of
What can only be given away
Come near!

Don't let your past define you

Don't let your past define you
Or what has gone
Determine what is yet to come
Do not assume that you can never change
For you are not merely
The sum of your parts
The end product
Of your story
All things can be made good
Don't let what has happened
Echo into the future
Thinking that what has been before
Will keep reoccurring
That history
Inevitably repeats itself
It is never too late
To start again
Don't anticipate disaster
When it is not
Lurking around the corner
Conclude that things
Can never be different
Or believe the lie
That there is no hope for you
What is done
Is finished
You can begin again
It is never too late
To start over

[44]

More than meets the eye

Not everything that happens makes sense
There is more to life
Than this world dreams of
Inexplicable moments
When it feels like
Something is calling us
Drawing us
Into an invisible dimension
Towards the centre of all things
Not everything that happens can be
Explained by science
Or unravelled by philosophers
There is more to life than meets the eye
Than what we can identify
With our senses
Are we merely
A bunch of atoms
Spinning about in space
From birth to death
Simply a speck in eternity
Then lost in the mists of time
Surely there is more to life
Than this

Running to the light

Cold and hard
Frozen
Lost in time and space
But running to the light

Defrosting slowly
Melting
Night by night
Standing in the light

Wide-eyed, dazzled
By Your bright shining
Exploding newness
Hope resurrected
Dumb-struck
Such awesome
Brightness
All enveloping, all encompassing
Incomprehensible
Vastness

Running to the light
I am renewed
I am reborn
Running to the light
I am transformed
I am alive
Running to the light
I'm running to the light

Time after time

I'm dizzy, still spinning
Not sure where I am
Like waking from a dream
When nothing's what it seems
Exploding with colours
Like fireworks in the rain
Like bubbles in the sun
I cannot hold them
Not what I expected
Uncharted territory
Life cannot be the same
Is this the end of me
Time after time
From my ashes You let me rise
From the debris of my life
You make something beautiful
Each time I fail
Each time I fall
You lift me up
out of the shambles of my life
Time after time
And You
Make all things new
In You
All things are new

Do not let the enemy

Do not let the enemy try
To squeeze you back into
The mould that he made for you
Long ago when he tried to determine your fate
And recreate you in his own likeness
Do not reopen the wounds that have been healed
Put back together what has been severed
Whisper again the lies
That have been unmasked
Or look back in anger
Over what has been forgiven
This mould is no longer for you
Not your habitation, your destiny
For now you belong in a wide place
A vast expanse of freedom
Where love is the beginning and the end
And everything in between
Where there are no more dark corners or shadows
But only light

Things that are sent to try us

Things that are sent to try us
Will happen when we least expect them
And catch us off our guard
So it's important
To stay awake
To remain alert
To always be on guard
Things that are sent to try us
Will easily disturb and annoy us
Easily upset and distract us
Cause us to wander off
In a direction that we had not
Actually intended to go
Cause us to lose our focus
To look away from what
Is most important
And to fix our gaze on anything, everything else
That is not Him

Guard your heart

Guard your heart
It is a treasure so precious
So valuable
Guard your heart
It is the very core of your being
Your centre
Guard your heart
For it is easily broken
Easily torn in two
Guard your heart
Do not cast it like a pearl
Before swine
Or let it be trampled on
With your dreams
Do not leave it for wolves
To devour
Or hand it over thoughtlessly
To another
This heart is yours
It can transport you, enraptured, to paradise
Or drown you in depths of sorrow
It can move you to heights of compassion
Or arouse you to intensities of anger
Guard your heart
It is yours to keep
And only yours to give away
Guard it well

Be careful where you build

Be careful where you build
For there are many treacherous places
That can be deceptive
For the builder
Who needs to have an eye
For a firm foundation
A solid structure
That will stand the test of time
Not all ground is fit for construction
A beautiful landscape
Can belie a safe position
Do not be taken in
By the lure of lush greenery
And balmy weather
Yet fail to consider
All that lies beneath
And not simply what is evident on the surface
Be careful how you build
Do not be in a tearing hurry
Or use mediocre materials
For cheapest is not necessarily best
This edifice needs to endure
Not collapse
At the first sign of a storm

Let your roots go down deep

Let your roots go down deep
Do not linger
In the shallow ground
Where the hot sun scorches and shrivels
Where the jungle of weeds
Chokes and constricts
And where the thorns and thistles
Snag and scratch
Do not stray on the path
Where the shadowy birds
Circling with an eye for an easy target
Swoop to snatch what is not rightfully theirs
Let your roots go down deep
Do not sojourn amongst the stones
Where there is no room to grow
No nourishment, no sustenance
Only the arid hardness of barren wastes
Let your roots go down deep
To the subterranean wells of fresh water
The life-giving deep cisterns
These you cannot see from the surface
But they are there
Oh yes, they are there
In the safe, dark places
Deep, deep down
Let your roots go down deep

Take care on the road

Take care on the road
For it is not as wide as you think
If you are not always fully alert
And do not keep looking
Where you are going
You may suddenly find that you are
No longer within
Its narrow confines
Take care on the road
For at times
It can be rough and steep
Many obstacles lie in the path
It isn't always smooth going or flat
As its way lies through rugged mountains
And down into unexpected valleys
Take care on the road
For it is long and winding
To reach the end
Takes dogged determination
And purposeful perseverance
The need to travel with the end in mind
Even though it is an end
That you cannot see
Do not lose your nerve
Bow down to discouragement
Or give in to the enticing calls
Of the world
Take care on the road

Here with me

I'm standing by the window trying to look through
If I stayed here long enough would I see you
You're in another heaven, in another world
You're closer than a hair's breadth, yet so far away

Shining with the angels, far too bright to see
I cannot get near you in your reality
Would I glimpse your brightness if I stayed right still
Everything suspended, wanting only you

You and me together, how could I not know
Nothing else now matters, nothing else but you
Looking through the window, I can see you there
Piercing through the darkness, lighting my whole world

Closer than my heart-beat, you're here
Always where I am, you're there
Always right beside me, you are
Closer than my breath, I can feel you near

Who is my neighbour

The one who stands beside me in the queue
The one who pushes past me in the line
The one who gives me sugar when I'm short
The one who throws an egg at my new car
The one who brings me flowers when I'm down
The one who hurls abuse out in the street
The one who comes from here and looks like me
The one who doesn't sound like what I do

Who is my neighbour
To whom should I show
Mercy and kindness
Patience and love
Who is my neighbour
To whom should I give
Support and assistance
Comfort and aid

Above
all else

Forgiveness

What a weight has been lifted off my shoulders
Has been lifted off my heavy heart
The oppression
That came from the darkness of my mind
The darkness of my spirit
Has been erased
Obliterated
All that was dirty
Was tainted
Has been washed clean
All that held me captive
Destroyed
All that lurked in the shadows
Has been chased away
A new day has dawned
A new beginning offered
Freedom to be
Freedom to grow
Freedom to move forward
Into all that had been
Prepared for me
From the start

Alive

Everything seems different now
Feels different
As if before
All was grey and drab
But now everything
Is dazzlingly, sensationally bright
Colours intensified
Senses heightened
Expectations elevated
The way ahead
No longer seems
Impossible to navigate
Blurred and shrouded in mist
Bursting into
This awesome newness
Excitement builds
A previously inconceivable
Anticipation of good things
Of hope restored
And life in all
Its fullness
Now, at last
I really am alive

Righteousness

The righteousness God seeks
Is not in respectable behaviour
The rectitude of your actions
Or the wealth of your good deeds
It is not found in numerous long prayers
The reverence of your worship
Or your engagement in prolonged fasts
This righteousness does not come
From a conformity to moral principles
A sound knowledge of the scriptures
Or devotion to a virtuous life
The righteousness God seeks
Is found in dwelling close to His heart
In listening to His voice
In understanding His mind
It is in throwing yourself
Onto His mercy
Where you can be washed clean in His blood
And become holy, as He Himself is holy

Love

Love endures forever
Nothing can remove it
Nothing can destroy it
Love will not
Cannot
Fail
All that is good, all that matters
Lies within its grasp
Love is the beginning and end
Of all things
It writes on our hearts
An indelible message
If we would only look
In our darkest moments
We would still see
It shining letters
Shouting out
Above all else
And let it gently
Recapture our hearts
Love believes in the good
Always expects the best
Always hopes for more
Always sees what could be possible
And holds on tight, in spite of everything
Through the darkness
Knowing that
A new dawn is just around the corner

Freedom

Freedom is a song gently stirring
Buried for a seeming eternity
A faint echo of a time long past
Now rustling, fluttering, rising through darkness
Until, welling up from deep within
It creates a tide that
Can no longer be quelled or resisted

From long lost, long forgotten places
Its song will arise once more
Bursting forth from locked cages
Breaking through chains
And smashing down walls
Flinging wide prison gates
Destroying the captivity of hopelessness
The paralysation of fears

Freedom ascends, roaring
Releasing raw emotion
Spawning joy indescribable
Its melody swelling louder and louder
Until nothing else can be heard
Above its tumult
Soaring to immense heights
To an expansive place, its home
There it cannot be recaptured
And hidden away once more
Freedom's song reverberates
Echoing from every hilltop
A song that will not die

Hope

From street corners
Its melodic cadences tumble
Down desolate alleys
Dancing over uneven cobblestones
Across oily puddles
And past dark and dingy doorways
Hope sings
Your warfare has ended
Your sin is pardoned

Hope sings
From the swaying tree tops
Its joyful chorale
Resounds across the cloudy skies
Cascading down every hill
Into each valley
Hope sings
The crooked places shall be made straight
And the rough places smooth

Hope shouts good tidings
From the mountain tops
Do not be afraid
Behold your God is coming
He does not grow faint or weary
And those who wait on Him
Will renew their strength
And rise up
As if on eagles' wings

Peace

Peace falls down like rain
A million glistening drops
Triggering life
Washing away every sadness
Every terrifying moment
Peace shines bright like stars
A billion twinkling explosions
Renewing hope
Ushering in a new dawn

Enveloping peace
Richly heavy
Like a brocade blanket
Nothing can escape its gentle caress
It's warm embrace
Covering every heartache
Every fearful thought
Bottomless peace
Nothing can fathom it
Beyond our understanding
Beyond our wildest dreams

Peace falls down like rain
In every distant corner
Through every open crack it runs
Bringing reversals of fortunes
As its unerring stillness
Wipes away
All that should be past and gone

Joy

Joy dances in the heart
From heart to heart it jumps
Flinging happiness from one
To another
Gladness growing
Generating an enduring elation
An expectation
Of high hopes
A prospect of paradise
No misery here
No gloomful glumness
No moody melancholy
Joy runs deep
It cannot easily be erased
Delighting in all that is good
It radiates an intense exhilaration
A conveyable excitement
Uplifting those it touches
Joy shines from each face
Making its presence known
Making its presence felt
With each touch
Of its warm embrace

Patience

Patience waits peacefully
Its calm composure
Demonstrates a diligent determination
Without agitation or alarm
Patience is not hurried or hasty
It is not irritable or easily irked
Patience is even-tempered
Not over excitable
And maturely manages
In challenging conditions
Its careful caution
Even in the most turbulent times
Shows strength of character
It reveals restraint
When others
Would go charging in
Patience knows that angry words
Do not receive rewards
That the fury of frustration
Will not hasten
An end result
It knows that, in the end
All will be well
And all manner of things
Will be well

Wisdom

Wisdom waits patiently for the right moment
Not rushing in where fools fear to tread
It soberly considers all the options
Purposefully weighing up each possibility
Giving due regard for its pros and cons

Wisdom recognises the opinions of others
Not forever wanting its own way
It does not scream loudly or act rudely
But seeks to act sensitively in every situation
Being mindful of experience and expertise

Wisdom always wishes to be reflective
Not believing that it knows it all
It searches out knowledge and expertise
Desirous of building on what has already been learned
Hoping to open up new horizons

Wisdom acts fairly, judges rightly
Behaves prudently, prepares carefully
It combats helplessness, defeats powerlessness
Operates shrewdly, brings understanding
Wisdom does not hide
It can be found by all who seek it
Its voice is plain to hear
For it shouts in the streets
And cries out in the marketplaces

Truth

Truth is not relative
It is not a figment of imagination
Something conjured up
Out of the heart or mind
Truth is not uncertain
It does not oscillate or fluctuate
Something that changes with changing times
Truth is not empty
It is not hollow, or devoid of meaning
Something beyond reason or wisdom
Truth is solid, certain, clear
Resounds through time
Belonging to forever
It brings clarity, revelation, hope
It points the way
And defines the journey
Truth stands firm
When other things have failed

Together

Where we belong
Is right here, right now
No longer separate, apart
But joined
Who we are
No longer two
But one
Greater than the sum
Of our individualities
Going forward in tandem
Two lives, one flesh
Two hearts, one voice
Such unity
Shouts from the rooftops
Calls to the desolate places
Runs down like oil
Over a weary land
Together we'll stand
Resolute in purpose
Firm against all foes
Strong in the storm
Steadfast in defeat
Together we'll go

Forward into the future
Sharing every precious moment
Every heart's desire
An open book
Grasping hold
Of our destiny
Holding fast
To hope poured out
Vision revealed
Knowing that nothing can destroy
Our eternal end

Stillness

In the stillness
In the quiet place
I find peace
In the silence
In the secret place
I find rest
In the calmness
In the private place
I find serenity

No restlessness here
No worry
Only tranquility
No agitation here
No fear
Only harmony
For here
Where You are
All is still
And You
Prince of Peace
Are all in all

Gratitude

Gratitude sparkles like sunshine
Radiating joy
Rousing thankfulness
It alights on every good thing
Every precious moment
Every kind word or deed
Acknowledging its appreciation
Of all things
The value
In all things
Gratitude does not complain
It does not react bitterly
To undesired events or situations
To thoughtless actions or callous deeds
Or retaliate with angry or coldhearted words
It does not trudge endlessly
Disconsolate and dispirited
Through the muddied puddles of the past
But gleams steadfastly
Through every storm and whirlwind
Knowing that they will pass
Gratitude responds graciously
Offering genuine appreciation
Giving thanks continuously
For every offering of life
In the sure knowledge that each
Makes a meaningful contribution
To life's song

Battle

This is no ordinary fight
Do not be naïve, unaware
Do not be oblivious
Of the battle that is raging, relentlessly
All around you
Of the brooding darkness
Encroaching
Insidiously creeping forward
Aiming to silently, unobtrusively
Obliterate all in its path
Until every light
Is extinguished
This enemy
Takes no prisoners
Leaves no survivors
In its wake
So do not carelessly picnic
In this war-zone
Unmindful of his intention
Of expansion
Wake up, wake up
Sound the alarm
Prepare to join the fray
Believing that this present darkness
Cannot endure
Forever

A glimpse of Heaven

Not of this world

He said that His kingdom
Was not of this world
And now
He has gone
Through the veil
To the heavenly places
Where He is enthroned
At the right hand
Of His Father

Our citizenship is in heaven
The curtain has been torn asunder
Where He has gone
We are now free to follow
An entrance into the throne room
Has been bought for us

The blood speaks

The blood speaks
I have loved you with an everlasting love
From the foundation of the world
The blood cries out
Your sins have been forgiven
And your iniquity pardoned
The blood announces
Your enemy has been defeated
And is bound in chains forever
The blood declares
Your warfare is over
And you may dwell in safety
The blood shouts
You are a new creation
A child of the Living One
The blood proclaims
There will be a new heaven and a new earth
The Lamb that was slain is on the throne forever

There's nowhere else I'd rather be

There's nowhere else I'd rather be
Gazing at breathtaking towering mountains
Or spectacular flaming sunsets
Walking across expansive silver sandy beaches
Or along lush verdant river banks
Swimming in balmy azure seas
Or riding on the deep face of a breaking wave
These are all nothing
Nothing
Compared to even one single precious moment
In Your presence

I would rather
Sit with You in heavenly places
Rest beside You at Your feet
Or even just stand at the doorway of Your dwelling place
Trying to peek in
Just to catch a glimpse
Of Your house
To experience a moment of eternity
For that one single fleeting moment
Is better than a lifetime anywhere else
For nothing
Nothing
Can compare with You

We cannot even begin to imagine

We cannot even begin to imagine
All that has been prepared for us
Even our wildest dreams
Cannot come close
To the reality
Of what will be

All that is now
May be hard to bear
The going may be tough
Or hopes lie about us in ruins
But remember
All that is now is not all that there is

All that will be
Is far more
Than the heart could imagine
Or the mind conceive
What has been prepared
Will surpass even our wildest
Most extravagant dreams
Our greatest hopes
Out of the breathtaking vastness of His love
He has done this

Echoes of Heaven

Do you not realise
That where you are standing
Exactly where you are
Is a thin place
A place of connectedness
Between Earth and Heaven
An access point
From Earth to Heaven
Be still, very still
Quieten your mind
And your pounding heart
Look very hard
Focus beyond the curtain
And you will see
Into the invisible world's realm
And catch a glimpse of Heaven
Listen very carefully
And you will hear echoes of Heaven
That small voice
Which is not in the earthquake or the fire
But is everywhere
Wherever we are
Right where we are standing
If only we would
Eliminate the tumult around and within us
The clamour of a thousand captivating voices
And stop long enough
To be able to hear

Streams in the desert

There are streams in the desert
That flow from the throne
The heart of the Father
To His children made known
And the life of the Spirit
That springs up within
Pours out to a thirsty world

There are pools of deep water
Refreshing and clear
The wounded and weary
Will drink and draw near
And the power of the Father
The love of the Son
Is shown to a hurting world

There are rivers of water
That run through the land
Green pastures and meadows
And trees at each hand
And your sons and your daughters
Sing and rejoice
Bringing hope to a weary world

Now let the wilderness rejoice
And all its streams make glad the nations
As they hear the song
They will rise and bless the King

Heavenly beings

These creatures
Inhabitants of the invisible world's realm
The space between worlds
Bear no resemblance whatsoever
To the imaginings of medieval painters
Or the wishful thinkings of well known singers
These creatures are
Awesome beyond words
Majestic beyond description
Powerful beyond understanding
Behold
Fire upon fire
Gold upon gold
Breathtaking brilliance, illuminating heavens
Penetrating darkness with overpowering light
Their worship, of the Lamb that was slain
Their song, to the Lion on the throne
Hold heaven enthralled
With their unbelievable beauty
And exceptional intensity
Yet these creatures
These wondrous, immortal, heavenly creatures
Long to know
The secrets of men
And yearn to hear
Salvation's song

Walking amongst the lampstands

His voice
Is like the roaring of a majestic waterfall
The crashing of mighty ocean waves
His speech
Reverberates, like the rumbles of thunder
Exults, like songs of a thousand choirs
His words
Sharper than any two edged sword
Penetrate deep into the very soul

And He, who uttered worlds into being
Who holds all things together
Is walking amongst the lampstands
The Light of the World
With eyes blazing like fire
And face bright as sun
And He, who sees all that can be seen
Knows all that can be known
Declares all that needs to be said
And His light
Is shining through the darkness
And cannot be extinguished
He has released its captives
And holds the keys of death and hell
The Light of the World
Who is walking amongst the lampstands
Has risen upon us

No more death

Not the end
But the beginning
So long-awaited
By a groaning creation
The time when tears
Are no longer necessary
Anxieties laid to rest
And death is dead
The door
Into the invisible world
Is opened up forever
Here, all is resplendent
Reversed, restored
Lambs and lions walk together
And guns and swords
Remade, as gardening tools
Here, healing can be found
In the leaves on the trees
And the sound of creation's song
Serenades every joyous heart
All things have been made glad
For the One who died
And is alive forevermore
Has declared the defeat of death
Has vanquished every enemy
Where He has gone
All can now follow

These trees

These trees are unlike any other trees
Standing there on the banks
Of the life-giving river
Bark rippling, aflame with a myriad of colours

That other tree
So long ago, in the garden
There, at the dawn of time
Its fruit enticing, delicious
Destined to deliver
The corruption of creation
And the mortality of mankind
Opening up a gate
Into dark places
We were not meant to explore
A doom encapsulated in every juicy bite

But these trees
These trees
Are for the hope of the world
The healing of the nations
In their leaves
Their leaves
A balm
To right wrongs
And to restore
All that had been lost
So long ago

The song

In the beginning
A song arose
From the far brightness of the heavenly places
It pierced the darkness
Of the universe
Bringing into being
All that was not
But now is
Its power gave rise to constellations
Stars and moons swept across skies
Its beauty gave rise to mountains
Fields and flowers painted across landscapes
And now
And still
Everything that is
Sings the song of heaven
Oceans roar, mountains shout
And the trees of the fields clap their hands
Even the stones are singing
For everything that exists
Gives praise
To the One
Whose song
Gave rise
To all

In the end

Such brightness
Is almost impossible to look at
To fix your gaze upon
A sea of clearest crystal
A city of glinting gold
Its foundations, its walls
Of precious stones
Its gates of pearl
The Light of the World Himself
Is its light
And therefore, there is no darkness there
No shadows, no obscurity
This indescribable, radiant brilliance
Has burned away
As if by fire
All that is not pure
All that is not true
Until in the end
There is only
The transcendent goodness
Of the Eternal One
Illuminating everything

ABOUT THE AUTHOR

Barbara lived, worked and worshipped in east London for over 30 years where she was a teacher, then head-teacher and teacher trainer, and on the leadership team of her local church, for which she was also the worship co-ordinator, before retiring and moving, more recently, to south west London. In addition to writing poetry, she has written many songs for use in church and school, including a musical for children, Mighty Moses. Barbara enjoys all kinds of music, visiting art exhibitions and museums and reading historical who-dunits.

Barbara's first book of poems, *The Stones are Still Singing*, is a vivid poetic narrative for Christmas and Easter, published in 2015 by Zaccmedia. More than just a collection of poems, it has been written for use in Christmas and Easter services, retreats, dance workshops, school assemblies and a range of church meetings and events.

The book is neither over simplistic for adults nor too difficult for children, but will add fresh inspiration into any public or private reading. The poems express the clarity and depth these special seasons bring. In some, the author has written as though in character, bringing a new perspective and intimacy to these most famous of stories.

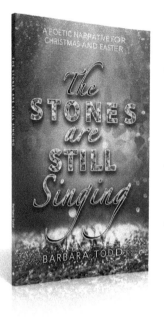

"This little book is a great resource for church leaders like myself who regularly plan special services and dramas for Christmas and Easter. The poems have great pace and rhythm (some are especially suitable for children to read) and they carry the events surrounding the birth and death of Jesus with imagination and flair, as well as biblical accuracy. Whether as a single poem read in a special service, or as part of an ongoing narrative over several days or weeks, they will be used again and again. I commend this resource to you."

THE STONES ARE
STILL SINGING
Barbara Todd
82pp / ISBN 9781909824768

– FAITH FORSTER,
Ichthus Christian Fellowship